Original title:
Greenhouse Grievances

Copyright © 2025 Creative Arts Management OÜ
All rights reserved.

Author: Maya Livingston
ISBN HARDBACK: 978-1-80566-615-8
ISBN PAPERBACK: 978-1-80566-900-5

The Trapped Flora's Lament

Oh, look at me, all dressed in green,
Chained to this pot, it's quite the scene!
I dream of wafting through fields so wide,
Instead, I'm stuck, with no place to hide.

The sunlight glints on my plastic dome,
But where's the breeze? I long for home!
My leaves are lovely, my blooms divine,
But darling, can someone please set me free to shine?

Roots Bound by Glass

My roots are weaving a tangled nest,
Trying to break out, I must manifest!
I tiptoe around like I'm in a dance,
But every step gets me stuck in a trance.

Walls all around, they just won't bend,
I swear this cage is a plant's worst trend!
Each day I stretch, but it's just a tease,
Oh, to escape would bring me such ease!

Dreams of Dappled Sunlight

Here I stand, longing for a sunbeam,
Yet in this box, I can only dream.
Oh, a touch of sky would be so grand,
Instead, I sip water from a tiny hand!

I hear the birds outside, chirping high,
While I'm just a chlorophyll-filled sigh.
If I could, I'd fly on a breeze carefree,
But alas, I'm stuck, can't you see?

Hidden Thorns Beneath the Canopy

Beneath my petals lies a clever ruse,
I hide my thorns, it's how I choose!
You think I'm sweet? Well, take a look,
These spikes are here, more than just a book!

In a cozy nook, I greet with charm,
But watch your step, I'll raise alarm!
With laughter and pricks, I dance on the floor,
Oh, the irony is hard to ignore!

Choking Vines of Expectation

In the corner, they twist with glee,
Hopes entwined, a wild spree.
Daily dreams climb up so high,
But struggle's the limit, oh me, oh my!

A tomato plant with big ambitions,
Promises ripe, with tasty renditions.
But all it yields, this leafy affair,
Is a salad of bugs and a pinch of despair.

The Sighs of Sheltered Blooms

Petals tremble in airy bliss,
Whispers of sun they seem to miss.
"Here's another cloudy day!"
They grumble low, but there they stay.

Caught in a pot, the daisies pout,
"What's the point? Let's just bail out!"
Yet still they smile at the rain,
Laughing softly, embracing the strain.

Unseen Ferns in the Shadow

Ferns in the corner, they plot and scheme,
"Where's the light?" they quietly beam.
"Perhaps a sticker that says 'Full Sun'?"
Beneath the shelf, they think it's fun!

Mold may rise from their hidden plight,
A fungus party by candlelight.
They drink up moisture, not a care,
While sneaking glances at the air!

Petals Weep in Stagnation

The blossoms droop, they're feeling blue,
"Send some breeze, it's overdue!"
A stillness thick as a summer's eve,
"Someone water us!" they plead and heave.

A cactus snickers, "I'm doing great!"
While gathered blooms debate their fate.
"Let's start a trend—of wilting grace!"
In this plant world, there's no sad face.

Echoes of the Overgrown

In corners wild, the weeds do dance,
Chasing sunlight like a romancing chance.
The herbs all giggle, the flowers complain,
As pests in tuxedos stalk through the lane.

The snails are slow, they're plotting their crime,
While ants play poker, oh what a time!
The gardener's sighs echo off the walls,
As he wrangles his way through delicate brawls.

Glass Walls and Grafted Hearts

Behind the glass, the plants all prattle,
With secrets whispered, they jest and rattle.
The cactus jokes about its pointy plight,
While roses blush as they flirt with the light.

In a pot so snug, the peppers all tease,
About how they'll spice up the next great breeze.
The tomatoes chuckle at their juicy fate,
As the basil plans a gourmet date.

Frustration in the Fertile Soil

The carrots sulk beneath the ground,
They dream of summers, lost and found.
The broccoli mutters, 'I'm too cool to cook,'
While radishes giggle in their leafy nook.

The earthworms wriggle, their dance is grand,
Plotting a takeover of the flower stand.
The daisies roll their eyes, oh what a fight,
In this patch of chaos, all's wrong but right.

A Garden's Cry for Freedom

The garden's alive with voices so bold,
From sunflowers groaning, to marigolds scold.
They yearn for a break from the trowel's grip,
Plotting a journey on a tissue-wrapped trip.

The herbs are prepared for a wild escapade,
To dance on the lawn, let their worries fade.
Yet as they conspire, the gnomes just sigh,
'Who knew our plants were destined to fly?'

The Glassbound Gloom

In a house of glass, it's warm and bright,
Plants wear sunscreen, a curious sight.
Bacteria overheat, they start to pout,
While flowers complain about the heat, no doubt.

Sweating veggies, oh what a mess,
Tomatoes blush, but it's no success.
Cucumbers grumble, "We're fried, you see!"
While peas just giggle, "It's not hot for me!"

The Fading Green

Once vibrant leaves turn a shade of gray,
Complaints about water, come what may.
"More sunlight, less drip!" the orchids all shout,
While succulents mumble, "Just chill out!"

Photosynthesis now feels like a chore,
"I miss the sun, just like before!"
But in their heart, they'd rather be free,
Than stuck on this plant pot jubilee.

When Fertile Souls Fade

Dirt gets clingy like an old friend,
Yet all these roots just can't pretend.
"Enough with the fertilizer, we want a break!"
Squeezed in the soil, they begin to ache.

"Do we water dance, or just sit here pouting?"
Herbs spill secrets, while they keep shouting.
"Botanical drama, it's quite absurd,
Who knew soil could gossip in every word?"

A Dance with Drought

The garden waltzes, but the soil is dry,
The daisies are thirsty, and they start to cry.
"Just a sip, please!" they plead with the hose,
While cacti snicker, "We're cool, who knows?"

Weeds break dance, take the watering can,
"Life is too short, be wild, be a fan!"
Bizarre ballet in the sizzling sun,
Flora united, their struggle is fun.

Sown Secrets of the Soil

In the dirt, whispers thrive,
Seeds tell tales, they contrive.
Worms gossip on a midnight spree,
Planting doubts about the pea.

Sunlight beams a mock surprise,
While carrots roll their beady eyes.
Tomatoes blush beneath the shade,
Plotting a fruit parade that's made.

The Strain of the Stalwart Stem

Little sprouts raise their tiny heads,
Complaining of the heavy beds.
Each leaf droops with a tired sigh,
Wishing they were birds to fly.

Stalwart stems do their best to stand,
But dream of a more exciting land.
Dance with breezes, toss and twirl,
Not stuck here, just in leafy whirl.

Bound Blossoms, Broken Dreams

Promises made in seed-filled hours,
Rosebuds trapped behind weak towers.
Each bloom hopes to reach the sky,
But naps too long and says goodbye.

A daisy argues with the vine,
'Give me sunlight, I'll be divine!'
Yet tangled up in jealous weeds,
The dreams burst forth, but sprout with needs.

Chlorophyll and Chained Aspirations

Chlorophyll dreams in shades of green,
Wishing to dance on a magazine.
But pot-bound roots have too much weight,
To twirl and spin, accept their fate.

In sunlight's glare, they plot and scheme,
To break the chains, to dare the dream.
Yet daily chores make them forlorn,
As they sigh and face another morn.

Reflections of Regret

In a world of lush delight,
The plants grow tall, oh what a sight!
Yet here I stand, a wilted fool,
Forgot the rules, forgot the cool.

The veggies mock with leafy cheer,
While I just sip another beer.
I swore to tend, oh, what a plight,
My garden's gone; it's a true fright.

The Dust Settles

Dust bunnies swirl like seasoned pros,
Hiding from my green-thumb woes.
I promise to clean, but I forget,
My plants just thrive on my regret.

The pots are cracked, the soil's dry,
The weeds spring up, oh me, oh my!
They laugh and dance in wild disarray,
While I just sit here and say, 'Okay.'

Tended but Tired

With watering can, I took my aim,
But every time, it's just the same.
The plants expect a spa retreat,
While I just offer them some heat.

Pruned and proud, I shed my tears,
For all these years, it's just my fears.
I buy them snacks, they ask for more,
Now I'm the meal they can't ignore.

Trapped in a Verdant Cage

Surrounded by the lushest greens,
I curse the day I saw those beans!
They grow with glee while I just stand,
Forget my dream of gardening grand.

With every sprout, I lose a chance,
To reclaim life and take a stance.
Here in my jungle, I can't escape,
These leafy friends, they plot and gape.

Rain on Stagnant Soil

Drip, drop, the raindrops tease,
But puddles form with utmost ease.
A dance of mud, oh what a sight,
In soggy boots, I shan't take flight.

The plants all sigh, too wet to grow,
They float around like seeds in throe.
No vines to climb, just sludge below,
A gardener's tale of woe, oh no!

The Anguish of Aspiration

I dream of blooms so bright and tall,
Yet ambitions stumble with a fall.
A seedling peeks, then hides in fright,
Like me on stage, too scared to light.

Fertilizer smirks, it's much too strong,
And my poor plants feel they've done wrong.
Their leaves are drooping, oh what a mess,
A horticultural game of chess!

Dreams Drowned in Dew

Each morning's grace brings morning dew,
But my plans are soggy, oh boo-hoo!
The blossoms dream of clearer skies,
Instead, they sigh and roll their eyes.

With watering cans and lots of hope,
I guide my green pals along the slope.
But come the flood, we are undone,
In dreams of sun, we had such fun!

Crumpled Leaves

Crumpled leaves, they wave goodbye,
With every gust, they seem to fly.
A crunch beneath my eager feet,
Such whispers of woes they repeat.

Once lush and green, now tales of dread,
They wish to sprout but lie instead.
"O gardener dear, please hear our plea,"
As I trip on roots and fall with glee!

The Stirring of the Still

In a cramped glass house, oh what a scene,
Plants out of hand, like a botanical dream.
Cacti plotting mischief, herbs in a band,
While tomatoes gossip, it's all quite unplanned.

Beetroot debates with the sweet potatoes,
Who's the funniest of their planty videos?
Lettuce is laughing, it's turning quite red,
Basil chimes in, 'You've lost your head!'

The sun shimmies down, it's quite the disco,
While flowers are shimmying like they're in a show.
In this leafy laughter, life's silly and bright,
In the garden of giggles, the future's alright.

Evacuating Eden

In a fruity forest, where apples once twirled,
Squirrels are scheming, it's chaos unfurled.
Peaches are rolling, all over the ground,
While strawberries shout, 'Get out of this town!'

Pumpkins are plotting a secret escape,
'Let's form a crew, we'll all need a cape!'
Carrots are carrot-ing away with great haste,
While grapes look on, a bit over-chased.

"Oh, the horror!" cried the beans in a whirl,
"Let's not get saucy, and laugh as we twirl."
Bananas go slipping, embracing the fun,
As they dance out of Eden, oh what a run!

Unwatched Wonders

In the world of the unwatched, plants stretch their roots,
As onions host parties in their leafy suits.
The daisies are dancing in a nightly spree,
Under the moonlight, they're wild and so free.

A carrot magician pulls radishes out,
"Look at my tricks!" he begins to shout.
The basil is baffled, and thyme's feeling bold,
As secrets unfold that were never foretold.

But watch out for spiders, with webs they'll ensnare,
A net for the garlic, but they just don't care.
In the chaos of nights, where whispers abound,
Unwatched wonders will always astound!

Whispers of the Weary

The weary plants sigh, in their leafy attire,
"Oh, to escape this sun's wild fire!"
The ferns are getting frisky, and the sunflowers droop,
While the mint throws a party, it's quite the hoop!

"Come join our dance!" the petunias invite,
"We're tired of waiting, let's party tonight!"
The peppers do salsa, the herbs shake it right,
While carrots just chuckle at their silly plight.

With whispers of joy, the garden unveils,
From weary to cheery, oh how it prevails!
In a world made of giggles, each plant sings its tune,
With laughter and lightness, they revel till noon.

Murmurs of the Mournful

In the garden, plants do weep,
Cucumbers dreaming, unable to sleep.
A squirrel stole my prized radish,
Now my salad feels quite rabid!

The roses pout in hues of gray,
Wondering why they're kept at bay.
With every weed that springs anew,
They plot revenge; it's quite a stew!

Lettuce sighs in leafy dread,
'Why can't we have some peace instead?'
The gardener trips, a mighty fall,
Tomatoes giggle, that's their call!

But in the chaos, laughter blooms,
As daisies plot with merry tunes.
In the soil, mischief stirs and sways,
A jolly garden, or so it plays!

The Seeping Sorrow

Oh, the thyme feels rather blue,
Complaining, 'Oh what can I do?'
The carrots argue, 'We're too sweet!'
While onions just cry in defeat!

Basil declares, 'I'm quite a star!'
Pesto dreams of flying far.
Yet here they sit, rotund and round,
With jokes about weeds all around!

The drip of water brings such a pout,
As rosebushes whisper, 'Get out!'
While vines conspire to spread some cheer,
Singing songs for all to hear.

Yet in this quagmire of plantly plight,
The bees buzz by, a joyful sight.
In every frown, a giggle hides,
Among the greens, the laughter rides!

Leafy Lamentations

Oh, the cabbages mope and grieve,
Like brooding teenagers, they believe.
'Why don't we get enough sunlight?'
They clutch their leaves and mock the light!

Spinach shouts, 'I'm no sad sack!'
While basil laughs, 'For me, no lack!'
Yet shadows creep, and temps do drop,
Their hopes of sun, a fickle flop!

The daisies laugh at all the frowns,
'Get a grip, you leafy clowns!'
Yet radishes pout in the dark,
Yearning for joy, a little spark!

But humor flows as watered as rain,
Laughter leaves the garden plain.
In every sigh, there's still some cheer,
Among the greens, fun's always near!

When Dreams Run Dry

In the plot where dreams once grew,
The carrots mutter, 'Is this true?'
With water gone, they cry, 'Not fair!'
Dandelions laugh, without a care!

The peppers fume in shades of red,
Wishing they could hop instead.
While herbs exchange sarcastic jibes,
Creating chaos, just for vibes!

One day it rains, and joy ignites,
The plants, they dance, oh what delights!
Every droplet's a sweet reprieve,
Nature's humor, weaves and weaves.

So let them grumble, let them play,
In every sprout, a new ballet.
For even when the dreams run dry,
Laughter sprouts and won't comply!

The Pleas of the Perishing

Oh dear sun, please don't shine so bright,
My leaves are wilting, what a dreadful sight.
Water me once, or twice if you please,
I'd rather not turn into a crispy breeze.

Dear bugs, keep off my tender shoots,
I've got no plans to be on your roots.
I'll wave my stems as a mighty flag,
In hopes you'll find a tastier snag.

So here I stand, with a droopy frown,
Craving a drink, I'm about to drown.
The soil's a desert, time's ticking fast,
Let's turn this garden back to a blast!

With a wink at the worms in the soil below,
I beg for a break from this nutrient woe.
Just sprinkle some love, a pinch of delight,
And I'll bounce back to green within the night!

Clinging to Hope

In this pot, I persist, oh so spry,
With dreams of rain and a brightened sky.
Though my leaves, they hang as low as they can,
I greet each morning—yes, I'm still the man!

A little sunburned, my edges all brown,
But I shall not mope, I shall not frown.
With a thumb-press of faith and a whisper of cheer,
I'll blossom all colors, just wait for the sphere!

The squirrels may nibble, the deer may prance,
But I hold my ground, I won't take a chance.
A taproot of courage in nutrient-pushed muck,
I'll rise up like a champion or test out my luck!

So here's to my fellows who share the sun's glow,
Let's dance in the breeze, let our energies flow.
With every new sprout, we gather our hope,
In this raucous riot, together we cope!

A Chorus of Corroded Vines

A twist here, a curl, oh what a fine mess,
These vines have gone wild and they're causing distress.
We prance and we sway, but we're tired and slow,
With every disheveled leaf, we put on a show.

Sprouting with humor, we tangle and weave,
Chasing the sun, oh, we never believe.
"What's that?" says the ivy, "Am I part of a joke?"
"To grow up this way, one could nearly choke!"

The trellis, it teeters, it moans with a sigh,
"Your weight is a lot! How much longer can I try?"
Yet we cling to our dreams, we're the life of the party,
With laughter and mischief, we're never too tardy.

So if you see us, tangled and spry,
Remember our song, let out a good cry.
For in every jest, in each hum and vine,
There's joy in our struggles, a twist so divine!

Pains of Photosynthesis

Oh, chlorophyll blues, what a tragic plight,
I'm craving some sun, and yet it's not right.
These photons are playing a game I can't win,
With stomata jammed shut, where do I begin?

The cycle's a hassle, I'm stuck in a rut,
Leaves working overtime—who put them on strut?
I transform, I produce, but who can relate,
When all of my troubles come down to debate?

With water too low and the roots feeling gray,
I dance with frustration, but still find a way.
For each little molecule, I shout with a grin,
"I'm more than a plant! I'm the light from within!"

So here in this chamber, where things seem absurd,
I'll laugh at my pains; they're just nature's word.
For as long as I'm green and I bask in the light,
I'll battle the issues, keep my spirit bright!

The Harvest of Unspoken Feelings

Tomatoes whisper secrets,
Eggplants tell their tales.
Zucchinis dance with shadows,
While the lettuce never fails.

The peppers blush at gossip,
Beans can barely hide.
By the time we serve dinner,
They've all taken a side.

Carrots stand in protest,
Roots all tangled tight.
"Why can't we be friends?" they cry,
As the herbs take flight.

But when the feast commences,
Not a veggie stays mad.
They all join in the laughter,
What a harvest we had!

Echoes in the Enclosed Eden

In a glassy little castle,
With vines that jest and tease,
Cucumbers giggle softly,
Tickled by the breeze.

The basil rolls its eyes,
At the mint's brazen show.
"Do you think you're so fancy?"
"Wait till the wind gets low!"

And there's a chorus of sighs,
When the carrots start to croon.
Even the radishes join in,
Singing 'Under the Moon'.

Yet every time they gather,
It all turns into jest.
No matter how they quarrel,
They're all still at their best.

Fractured Foliage

Leaves in disarray, oh dear,
What chaos in the patch!
A basil leaf lost its mind,
And flipped into a match.

The violets told the daisies,
"Don't you dare grow tall!"
While the ferns cracked up laughing,
And tried to hide it all.

Carrots juggling beetles
Wore hats made of spun yarn.
A crowd of puzzled veggies,
In the midst of this charm.

But every laugh and bicker,
Was worth a thousand trips.
For in this quirky garden,
They all embraced their quirks!

Tethered Roots

Tangled roots beneath the soil,
Whisper tales of woe.
"Why are we stuck here?" they joke,
"We could be on a show!"

With feet stuck in the mud,
The carrots start to pout.
While dancing dandelions,
Are not trapped in this route.

The beans climb up the trellis,
In hopes of breaking free.
But really they just laugh about,
How wild life could be.

So tethered yet so happy,
They flourish side by side.
In their little patch of humor,
There's nowhere left to hide!

Fettered Spirits

Oh, the thyme was feeling trapped,
With the chives just rolling eyes.
"You think you're the best herbs?"
"Oh please, don't be so spry."

The sage began its ramble,
Spouting nonsense, quite absurd.
While the dill just stood there chuckling,
"Have you ever tasted curd?"

Yet as the sun sets slowly,
Laughter fills the air.
Even with their petty spats,
They found they truly care.

In their pots of wise-cracking,
Fettered spirits soar.
And with each pot of soil,
They're anchored evermore!

The Withering Heartbeats

In a garden where laughter grows,
Plants dance, but oh, how it shows!
With tangled roots and snarky blooms,
They laugh as sunlight slowly looms.

Petunias gossip, so bright and bold,
Sipping dew while tales unfold.
Each leaf a secret, every stem a jest,
They poke fun at the weeds, oh what a fest!

A cactus claims it feels so fine,
While drooping daisies sip on wine.
With puns so cheesy, they twirl and sway,
In this patchwork realm, they frolic and play.

But when the rain, it starts to pour,
The giggles fade, they cling for more.
Yet after storms, their laughter breaks,
As sunshine returns, the garden wakes!

Weeds Among the Wailing

Among the blooms is chaos today,
Weeds with jokes, they love to play.
They sprout right next to roses fair,
Causing sighs and mock despair.

Oh, dandelion with a wily grin,
You think you're sly, but I'm here to win!
Your roots are deep, your humor crass,
Yet how you make the flowers laugh en masse!

Chrysanthemums roll their eyes in glee,
As thistles tell tales of woe so free.
Oh how they wound with laughter's knife,
In the tangled tales of planty life.

But watch out dear weeds, the pruners near,
Their scissors gleam, it's time to fear.
You jest too much, but here's the twist,
The laughter lingers where joy persists!

The Ego of an Everbloom

A sunflower struts, it's quite the sight,
Basking in praise from morning light.
With petals wide and a poppin' stance,
It claims, 'I'm royalty, let's dance!'

The roses scoff, 'Oh, what a frame!'
While violets whisper, 'What a shame!'
For in the shadow, hush whispers float,
As ego blooms on a leaf-like coat.

Yet in the breeze, a daisy laughs,
'Oh dear bloom, look at your halves!
For beauty fades as daylight wanes,
While weeds embrace the summer rains!'

But pride remains in fragrant air,
The everbloom doesn't seem to care.
It blossoms forth with tales so bright,
Ignoring whispers, basking in light!

Strangled Growth

In tangles twining, oh what a sight,
With vines of chaos, a comical plight.
Each leaf a bicker, every bloom a feud,
They strangle laughter, oh what a rude!

The tomatoes boast, 'We bear the weight!'
While cucumbers giggle, 'Don't seal your fate!'
Yet zucchini woes and squash debates,
Turn garden plots into hilarious fates.

As weeds conspire, they plan their heist,
To choke the blooms with a brazen slice!
But laughter bubbles, gardens grow wide,
In this tangled mess, joy will abide.

For every chokehold comes a grin,
And every struggle, a chance to win.
In strangleholds of green delight,
The garden chuckles, bursting with light!

The Silent Sway of Leaves

In a house of glass, they sway and shake,
Whispering secrets, for goodness' sake.
Photosynthesizing with flair and glee,
While plotting how to escape their decree.

The sunbeams tickle, the shadows play,
Cacti in the corner just can't find the way.
Lettuce giggles in her leafy domain,
As peppers ponder, 'Is this all in vain?'

A spider plant lounges, saying with pride,
"I'm the life of this party, they can't override!"
The vines are climbing, a bold little act,
While the petunias gossip, 'Is that a fact?'

But one rogue sprout peeks from the top,
Shouting to all, "I won't let this flop!"
With a flourish and twist, they dance with delight,
In this glassy abode, oh what a sight!

Shadows of the Stunted

Under the lights, they struggle and groan,
Silly little plants, feeling all alone.
A tomato tripped on his own tangled vine,
While the basil snickers, 'Just wait for the thyme.'

In a crowded corner, they all seem to pout,
"Why did that seed think it could sprout?"
Moss laughs softly, hiding his face,
"We're all just stuck in this tight little space."

The ferns are fidgeting, their fronds all a-twist,
Wishing for space, oh how they insist!
But behind them a flower shouts with pure cheer,
"I'll grow out of this, I've nothing to fear!"

With each new day, they yearn for the sun,
Dreaming of freedom and having some fun.
Yet here in this pot, they stay close-knit,
Creating a ruckus! Oh, just a bit!

Cracks in the Structure

In a dome made of sadness, a crack did appear,
Plants peered outside, hoping for cheer.
A tiny sprout squeaked, 'I swear I saw light!'
While ferns whispered softly, 'That's quite a sight!'

The framework creaks, a symphony of woes,
As plants roll their eyes at the garden hose.
"Oh why must we stay? Can't we go explore?"
Cried a cactus who yearned for much more!

Amidst the commotion, a wise old rose said,
"Don't fret little pals, we've got dreams in our head!"
"We'll stretch and we'll bend, we'll find our own way,
Together we'll grow like it's our birthday!"

With roots entwined, they giggled with glee,
"What lies beyond will be quite the spree!"
So they danced in the shadows, cracked walls content,
In a world full of dreams, they felt quite well-meant.

The Unheard Echoes of Growth

In the quiet corners, they whisper and sigh,
The sprouts are dreaming of reaching the sky.
But lettuce gets nervous, 'I'd rather just stay',
While zinnias shout, "Let's fly far away!"

A tiny little seed, so bold and so spry,
Wonders aloud, 'Can we reach for the high?'
Though the soil is cozy, a little snug,
The daisies chuckle, 'You're just a young bug!'

Sunshine spills laughter over silken leaves,
Frolicking freely, they weave what they believe.
"Just take a deep breath, feel the warmth of the sun,
If you think of the garden, we just might have fun!"

And all the while, the shadows stand still,
Listening close to the whispers and thrill.
For in this wild dance of roots and of greens,
The echoes of growth are woven in dreams.

The Weight of Unyielding Light

In a sunroom, plants dance tight,
Reaching out for beams so bright.
But too much warmth can take a toll,
Squished leaves near a window's shoal.

Humidity's a fickle friend,
Dripping dreams that never end.
Potted pals in a race to grow,
Whisper secrets the sun won't know.

Late-night snacks go to their head,
Fruits that dream of leafy bread.
Oh, the weight of light so grand,
Bowing blooms just can't withstand!

But we chuckle through our plight,
Under the glow of day's delight.
For in this jungle, wild and free,
There's laughter shared in greenery.

Tendrils of Tension

Tendrils twist in a clumsy dance,
Reaching high like a vine's romance.
Yet one wrong step, and down they go,
Leaving leaves in a tangled show.

When watering spills turn to floods,
We're rescuing friends from their muddy thuds.
They scream for help; no time to pout,
A plant-parent's life is often a drought.

With every stretch, they scrape the ceiling,
A game of limbo, oh, what a feeling!
Yet in their struggle, we find the glee,
Of tangled greens and comedy.

So here's to vines and their crazy game,
A giggling riot, never the same.
In our tiny world of planty care,
Sometimes we snort — what a wild affair!

Harbored Hopes

In pots of dreams, we plant our goals,
With visions of greens and leafy strolls.
But watch them sprout; expectations soar,
Then flop like a fish that's washed ashore.

Sprouting hopes, like confetti tossed,
Forgotten while chasing the petty lost.
Fickle ferns and moody moss,
Wink at me just to show who's boss.

When seedlings break out, I cheer and sing,
Each little leaf feels like a king.
Yet one brown edge can set the tone,
And suddenly I'm calling a groan.

Still, I harbor hopes much like a craze,
In this garden circus, it's just a phase.
With every sprout, a tale unfolds,
Of future blooms, with laughter it holds.

Forgotten Flowers

In a corner, a floral mess,
Once a garden, now a guess.
Forgotten blooms with stories old,
Still whisper secrets, not yet told.

Petals curled like a tired sigh,
Wondering when was their goodbye.
A lonely pot with a faded hue,
Biding time, just waiting for dew.

Mismatched pots share stories grand,
Of sunshine days and soft, sweet land.
Yet we laugh 'til we shed a tear,
For blooms of laughter, not a fear.

So raise a glass to the lost bouquet,
In dusty corners, they still sway.
Amidst the weeds, a beauty shines,
Forgotten glory, in tangled lines.

A Prism of Pressed Petals

In a book of memories we keep,
Pressed petals sigh from their slumber deep.
A rainbow waits for a gentle breeze,
Yet all they do is take their ease.

Captured colors, once bold and bright,
Now looking tired, yet holding tight.
Their tales of blooms long lost to time,
Bring forth a giggle, a simple rhyme.

The little ones giggle at their plight,
As petals whisper of the light.
They dream of days when rebels flew,
Now stuck on pages, much like glue.

So let us cherish this muffin pan,
Of flowers frozen by childlike plan.
In every crease, a joke unfolds,
A prism holds the laughter — all that gold!

When Vines Weep

In the corner, a spider spins,
While the herbs argue, loud chagrins.
Tomatoes sulk, feeling so quite low,
Complaining about the seeds they sow.

Weed party rages, they wear a crown,
Declaring war on the local town.
'Let us grow wild!' the daisies cheer,
While the daisies complain about being near.

Mildew laughs as it sneaks around,
Disguised in the dirt, it won't be found.
'No more sunlight, let's play in gloom!'
As the broccoli shouts, "Let's dance in bloom!"

So as the vines weep from overdue rains,
The garden giggles at its own pains.
With laughter and sighs, they bloom and jest,
In this merry mess where we all invest.

Fractured Roots

Roots tangled up in a silly tangle,
They grumble and pout in a lighty jangle.
Basil's mad because mint's so bold,
While celery claims, "I'm far too old!"

Rhubarb insists it knows best of all,
But cucumbers laugh at this pompous call.
"Just look at your leaves, all droopy and bent,"
Yells a pepper who's feeling quite content.

A sunflower pokes its head in the fray,
With petals all bright, it wants to play.
"Stop with your bickering, come share a space!"
And the bickering halts, though not without grace.

Now laughter erupts in the tangled mess,
Roots finally find some calm to bless.
For in their jests and collective strife,
They grow together, a comedy of life.

Light Through Frosted Glass

Behind the panes where shadows dance,
Plants squint and glare, given half a chance.
"Where's the sun?" cries a thirsty bloom,
While cacti poke fun from their prickly loom.

The orchids whisper, dressed in flair,
"Why do the daisies think they're rare?"
And as the light filters, hues collide,
Peonies blush and take it in stride.

The ferns giggle at the tomato's plight,
Stuck behind glass, it longs for the light.
"Come outside!" croaks the frog from the bog,
"Join us in sunshine, and dance like a fog!"

So under the frost's gently warming haze,
They plot their escape in the meandering maze.
With humor as warmth, they break the glass wall,
Together they thrive, they answer the call.

The Burden of Blossoms

Petals tangle in a turbulent dance,
Whining for water, oh what a chance!
"I'm too heavy!" the peony cries,
While lilacs just laugh with their purple sighs.

The daisies complain of their sunken heads,
With arguments rising, like garden beds.
"Oh dear me, look at these bugs!" they bleep,
"Who knew that blossoms caused such a heap?"

The roses huff, all dressed in their best,
"We're burdened by beauty; we need a rest!"
As each flower flops in the afternoon heat,
They share silly tales of their floral defeat.

Yet through the giggles and splashes of hue,
They root for each other, as blossoms do.
With each little fumble and bloom that's absurd,
They laugh and they grow—nobody's deterred!

A Symphony of Withered Petals

In a world of plants that pout,
They gather round, with nothing stout.
Lettuce carpools in despair,
While the broccoli loses its hair.

Tomatoes grumble, losing their zest,
Cucumbers complain, 'We need a rest!'
A sprout shouts, 'Look at my flop!'
'Hey, don't fret, at least we're not corn on the cob!'

The herbs all agree, it's a losing race,
A basil's bad day turned into a disgrace.
The thyme's running out, the jokes flow like sap,
Yet in this chaos, they still take a nap.

As petals wilt, laughter rings true,
In this garden, hilarity brews anew.
With laughter and sighs, they carry the tune,
And dance in the shadows all night 'neath the moon.

The Suffering Sapling

Once sprouted bright, now sad and forlorn,
A sapling sighed, 'Why was I born?'
'Watered too much, or too little today?
I'm more confused than a child at a buffet!'

With roots all tangled, it pleaded aloud,
'Can someone help? I feel so cowed!'
A worm said, 'Chill, you're no laughingstock,
Just hang in there, and let the sun clock!'

It looked at the sky, said 'Make it snappy,
I'm feeling more droopy than old, cranky nappy.'
But rain decided to play a prank,
Dousing dreams of a mighty oak plank!

Through days of doubt, it learned to poke fun,
For life in the soil shines brighter than sun.
'If I can't be grand, then I'll just be cool,
A chill little sapling, breaking every rule!'

Beneath the Lattice of Grief

Beneath a lattice, the vines intertwine,
They conjure complaints over sips of brine.
'I thought I was a star,' says the snap pea bold,
'Turns out my glory is just a tale retold.'

The squash are sulking, draped in gray sheets,
'We wanted to shine, not rot in our beats!'
Eggplant, feeling quite bruised by the jibe,
Said, 'Look at us, ripe for an attic tribe!'

With leaves in a tussle and stems all a-flare,
'At least we're not cabbages, bereft of flair!'
'But can you imagine a world so bland?
We could debut a comedy act so grand!'

So within their lattice, they conjure their jest,
In this garden stage, they aim for the crest.
Taking pride in the mess, they laugh despite strife,
Finding joy in the chaos, that's the crux of life.

Seasons of Stagnation

The seasons come, and the plants stand still,
'Are we growing or just getting our fill?'
The daisies whisper, 'Is this all a game?
Or just a long wait for a turn in the flame?'

The carrots feel stuck, deep in their plot,
'If we move one inch, do we get what we sought?'
'Just root for the best, and maybe a bit of sun,
Stagnation's a tangle, but we'll have some fun!'

With flowers that bicker, and highs that revel,
They concoct a plan, a botanical revel.
'We'll dance through our drama, as though on cue,
If the world won't budge, then we will break through!'

So in their delay, they craft a new glow,
For laughter and joy, let the good times flow.
In a scene of stagnation, hilarity breeds,
A garden of joy from the most tangled weeds.

The Discontent of the Dappled Glade

In the bright dappled light we stand,
Plants waving hands, and demanding a band.
"More space!" they whisper, with a flounce and a sigh,
Yet no one can hear under this clear plastic sky.

The lettuce is strutting, the broccoli groans,
Their dreams of the wild whispered in tones.
"Let us out!" they mutter with a leafy pout,
But then who will water when the sun's out?

The peppers are plotting a grand escape,
Wearing their green coats, with plans they will drape.
"We'll slide past the windows, just wait and see!"
But all of their schemes end in slops and in glee.

So here in our garden, we laugh and we muse,
At the grumpy thyme, and the petulant blues.
In a home where the veggies complain with a grin,
We cherish the chaos, let the antics begin.

Esperance in Enclosed Spaces

Oh the herbs here are plotting a getaway scheme,
With basil and mint dreaming up ways to redeem.
Reaching for sunlight, they stretch and they fuss,
"This box just won't do! It's a plant prison bus!"

Cucumbers in corners, so close but yet far,
Whispering softly, "We should ask for a car!"
"Take me to the farmer's market by noon!"
They giggle in shadows, beneath the bright moon.

Tomatoes are laughing, with their round bumpy winks,
Plotting a caper with the little pink clinks.
"We'll roll down the lanes if we just find a way,"
And the radishes shout, "Let's make it today!"

Yet as tension rises, the peas join the fray,
"We're comfy right here, let's munch and delay!"
And who can resist, when they're all in a spin?
In these delightful confines, it's hard not to grin.

Unraveled Vines of Identity

The vines are confused in their tangled embrace,
"Who's who in this mess? What a chaotic space!"
With twists and with turns they can never align,
Saying, "I thought I was grape, but I'm feeling like pine!"

Roses are rolling, with petals unkempt,
"What's with the fuss? We're all just exempt!"
They prance in the soil with a frothy delight,
While the daisies just giggle, saying, "What's wrong with white?"

The squash had ambitions to grow far and wide,
Yet clings to the fence, where its hopes often hide.
"A throne I could have, among fruits of renown!"
But stuck in this bed, they just frown and sit down.

With laughter that dances in breezy refrains,
These leafy divas declare their own claims.
In the tangled confines, they bicker and play,
Embracing the chaos, come what may!

The Moisture of Regret

A watering can leaks with a clatter,
Soggy soil makes plants a bit fatter.
I tried to nurture the seeds that I sowed,
But they laugh at my efforts, my garden's a load.

The sun comes out, the weeds dance in glee,
I'm knee-deep in chaos, oh woe is me!
Tendrils of ivy invade my good space,
They think they're fashionistas with all that lace.

Potted herbs turn into a jungle quite wild,
Basil gets sassy, the parsley's a child.
Each time I prune them, they shudder and moan,
My rosemary's now more like a groaning old crone.

Rain clouds come calling, oh what a downpour,
I slip on my sandals, I trip and I swore.
Yet in this madness, a chuckle I find,
Plant life is silly, and so am I, blind.

Suffering in the Shade

The sun's blazing high, but shade's my defense,
Under a big leaf, I sit in suspense.
A snail on my lettuce, oh what a sight,
He claims it's his club, and I'm not invited right.

Lettuce and spinach, they gossip, they sigh,
They think they're the stars, and I am the fly.
Dandelions giggle, with their yellow crowns,
While I'm just here wearing my frown of brown.

Swinging on swings made of tangled up vines,
The cucumber's bickering, "Who gets the fines?"
The sunbeams send whispers, too hot to be real,
Shade's where the drama unfolds with a squeal.

Oh how I wish I could make them all cease,
But plants can't keep quiet, they're always at peace.
So here I will stay in my leafy retreat,
A spectator of chaos, my shade's a sweet seat.

Borders of Blooms

In beds of bright colors, my flowers collide,
The tulips in red just won't let it slide.
Roses and daisies share whispers of gossip,
While pansies throw parties and take it as profit.

Bees buzz around, like they own the whole place,
Their pollen negotiations, oh what a chase!
Fleeting friendships between petals and stems,
Jealousies brewing like overcooked jams.

The daffodils boast in their golden attire,
While violets sulk, feeling less than desired.
Each bloom is a diva, a tale to unfold,
Their roots tangled deep in the drama they sold.

Yet in this cabaret of colors and scents,
A comical view of the world that commences.
Nature's own sitcom, with laughter and cheer,
In the borders of blooms, absurdity's near.

Tethered in Time

Clock ticks away, I'm stuck in the dirt,
My plants have grown wise, I'm feeling unhurt.
They say 'Time is a sprout,' and 'Patience — a bloom,'
But I just want snacks while I sit in this room.

With every green leaf, my patience takes flight,
But give me some chips! It's a planty delight.
"Oh, where's that tomato?" I mumble and pout,
While blooms roll their eyes, "You should chill out!"

The fragrance of thyme drifts through the air,
Whispers of cilantro, "You're too much to bear!"
Yet here I remain, with my shovel and spade,
In this riveting scene, where realities fade.

So tethered in time, with a humor so bright,
My garden's a circus, my joy takes its flight.
In pots of delight, with each vine I unwind,
The comedy flourishes, and so do I — blind.

Silent Scream of the Succulent

In the corner, a cactus sighs,
Dreaming of water, beneath blue skies.
With parched limbs, it stands tall,
Whispering secrets to the wall.

The aloe rolls its leafy eyes,
"Another day, another sun," it cries.
While ferns just gossip, twirling about,
"Did you hear what that lily's about?"

The pot-bound sage grows a bit rounder,
Plans escape routes, schemes to be fonder.
With each passing hour, it twitches and shakes,
Yearning for adventure, some fun for its sake.

But in this still room, oh what a bore!
The dust settles thick, and the plants just snore.
Yet every now and then comes the day,
When the sun breaks forth and the colors play.

The Dichotomy of Bloom and Bane

A flower stood tall, bright and bold,
While a weed next door did something untold.
"Look at me here, I'm the best in show!"
The flower flaunts, with a vibrant glow.

The weed just chuckles, roots deep in the muck,
"Sweet bloom, you're stuck; I've got all the luck!"
With tangled vines and a charming flair,
It stretches wide without a care.

Petals are peeking, all prim and neat,
While thistles surround, ready to greet.
"Watch your step, darling!" they call in glee,
"Your charm's just a cover—a foe, not a friend to me!"

Such a ruckus unravels in the patch of green,
Where beauty and chaos form a strange scene.
Two worlds colliding, both wild and tame,
Nature's sweet jest, a glorious game.

A Garden's Soliloquy

Oh, the daisies dance in the sunlight bright,
While the weeds conspire, just out of sight.
"Come join us, dear bee!" they buzz and plead,
Yet, pollen's a game and they'll take the lead.

The carrot murmurs, "What a waste of a day!
Everyone's growing, but I'm stuck in my way."
Wistfully dreaming of the plate's grand design,
"I wanted to be a star, served with red wine!"

While radishes snicker, buried in gloom,
"Keep digging, dear friend, there's always more room."
An outburst erupts with a leafy shout,
"There's life underground, when the world's in doubt!"

And so they all chatter, both bold and shy,
Life in the garden, oh me, oh my!
Underneath moonlight, less divine is the vow,
That tomorrow will come, while they still just grow.

Toxic Tendencies

In the corner lurks a plant of dread,
With leaves so shiny, a humble bed.
"Touch me, I dare you," it seems to tease,
While nearby daisies just tremble in the breeze.

The wise old fern whispers in the dark,
"Don't trust that beauty; it's full of a spark!"
Yet clueless critters come in for a sip,
"Oh, it's so lovely," they say, losing grip.

With sparks of mischief, the plant takes a bow,
"I'm the life of the party, who cares how?"
But underneath charms lies a story untold,
For once they get too close, it'll be bold.

So guard your hearts, take heed of the scene,
Where the charming and cute are often unseen.
A garden can play tricks, both fun and absurd,
With toxic snares cleverly interworded.

The Hothouse Haunting

In the garden, ghosts of weeds,
They dance around in fancy beads.
The flowers bloom, while I just stare,
Did one of them put glue in my hair?

Those tomatoes mock with their red glee,
As I ponder why I can't seem to see.
The peppers plot with villainous glee,
Is that a shadow? No, it's just a pea!

The squash squabbles when I turn my back,
And every sprout is on the attack.
I swear I heard them laughing loud,
As I stumbled through the leafy crowd.

So here I stand, among my foes,
With plants conspiring to dethrone the toes.
But I'll keep planting, for what it's worth,
In this haunted realm of tender earth.

The Breath of Irony

In a world of plants that seem so wise,
My seedlings snicker while I despise.
They grow like ninjas, swift and spry,
   While I trip over pots and sigh.

The basil winks with fragrant charms,
   While I defend my clumsy arms.
Cucumbers giggle, hanging in place,
They know it's me who's lost the race.

A flock of leaves, they whirl around,
As I chase a rogue root that's found.
"Oh silly gardener," they seem to chant,
"Next year, sweet friend, please just plant a plant!"

But here I am, a funny sight,
With trowel in hand, ready to fight.
They won't defeat this silly fool,
For next week's planting is the real rule!

Ties that Bind and Break

With vines that twine and twist for fun,
They weave my plans, then come undone.
I thought I'd trained them, strong and neat,
But they conspired in the summer heat.

"Just hold it still," I said with glee,
Yet they dove for freedom, wild and free.
I tied them down with every string,
But plants don't care for royal bling!

A trellis promised, strong and grand,
Yet they dismantle, bold and bland.
"Stand tall, dear beans!" I cried in vain,
They laughed and flopped, a true disdain.

Oh, ties that bind, and yet they break,
In this wacky plant shindig, what a mistake!
Collapsing dreams of garden grand,
Next year, I'll just plant a cactus strand!

Asperity in the Afternoon Sun

Under the sun, my plants just grumble,
As I fumble through a summertime tumble.
The lettuce sulks, the carrots pout,
What's with this heat? They want to shout!

"Not another moment," the flowers plead,
"Get us some shade, or we won't succeed!"
And here I am, iced tea in hand,
While daisies plot a turning strand.

The squash complain of daily plight,
They dream of winter, oh what a sight!
While I'm left singing songs to the weeds,
Their whispers echo, "We've planted our seeds."

So, here's to my garden, all grumpy and bold,
Each plant has stories that must be told.
In this sunny saga of leafy despair,
We laugh together—there's magic to share!

Whispers in the Glass

In a castle made of glass,
Plants gossip with a sass.
Tomatoes claim they're ripe and red,
While basil dreams of being bred.

Cacti tease the soft green ferns,
"You're just jealous of our spurns!"
Sassy petals, leaves that prance,
In this place, they love to dance.

Lettuce complains, 'I'm stuck in here!
Bored of sunlight, give me beer!'
But all they get are watering cans,
And lettuce leaves that make no plans.

Behind the glass, laughter swells,
In verdant jail, they weave their spells.
Growing grumpy, fun takes flight,
In whispers green, they crave the night.

Flora's Lament

A flower cried, 'Oh woe is me!
Why must I sit? Let me be free!'
Sunflowers seek the sun's embrace,
While daisies dream of outer space.

The thyme grumbled, 'I should be spice,
But here I am—no herb's quite nice!'
Petunias pout, their colors bright,
'Let us out, we wish to fight!'

Oh, the ferns, they twitch and twist,
Gossiping of their chlorophyll mist.
"Why are we stuck? Let's break some glass!
And go back to our wild green grass!"

In every pot, a grumpy tale,
These leafy spouts who wish to sail.
So hear their woes, and giggle too,
For flora's wit is just for you.

The Caged Canopy

Under a roof of glass and air,
Trees are tall but filled with despair.
"Why can't we roam the forest floor?
I miss the breeze, I want to soar!"

Leaves are grumbling, branches sass,
"Life's a joke, this ain't no class!"
The oak says, "I should be a ship,
Sailing waves, instead I trip!"

Vines are tangled in their woe,
"Far away from earth, you know!
We're neat and green, but oh so bored,
A wildlife tale we can't afford!"

So in their cage, they bide their time,
Plotting escape, they make a rhyme.
With laughter loud, they find a way,
To turn their gloom into a play.

Beneath the Sheltered Sky

Underneath this glassy dome,
Plants have gathered, far from home.
Begonias sigh and say, 'Oh dear,
When will we get our chance to cheer?'

Chives are chanting 'Let us out!'
While ferns just whisper, 'That's a doubt.'
The cress makes jokes, a leafy clown,
While violets pout, feeling down.

Help wanted: a gardener mad,
To make life fun, or at least not sad.
But all they get is sunny rays,
And hours of the same old plays.

In their pine-scented little fief,
They plot their way to rebel relief.
With every leaf and every bud,
They'll escape this too-perfect flood.

www.ingramcontent.com/pod-product-compliance
Lightning Source LLC
Chambersburg PA
CBHW071833160426
43209CB00003B/285